Congressional Research Service
Informing the legislative debate since 1914 _____

Coast Guard Polar Icebreaker Modernization: Background and Issues for Congress

Ronald O'Rourke
Specialist in Naval Affairs

July 1, 2014

Congressional Research Service

7-5700

www.crs.gov

RL34391

Summary

The Coast Guard's FY2013 budget initiated a new project for the design and construction of a new polar icebreaker. The project received $7.609 million in FY2013 and $2.0 million in FY2014. The Coast Guard's proposed FY2015 budget requests $6 million to continue initial acquisition activities for the ship.

Coast Guard polar icebreakers perform a variety of missions supporting U.S. interests in polar regions. The Coast Guard's two existing heavy polar icebreakers—*Polar Star* and *Polar Sea*—have exceeded their originally intended 30-year service lives. *Polar Star* was placed in caretaker status on July 1, 2006. Congress in FY2009 and FY2010 provided funding to repair it and return it to service for an additional 7 to 10 years of service; the repair work was completed and the ship was reactivated on December 14, 2012. On June 25, 2010, the Coast Guard announced that *Polar Sea* had suffered an unexpected engine casualty; the ship was unavailable for operation after that. The Coast Guard placed *Polar Sea* in commissioned, inactive status on October 14, 2011.

The Coast Guard's third polar icebreaker—*Healy*—entered service in 2000. Compared to *Polar Star* and *Polar Sea*, *Healy* has less icebreaking capability (it is considered a medium polar icebreaker), but more capability for supporting scientific research. The ship is used primarily for supporting scientific research in the Arctic.

With the reactivation of *Polar Star*, the operational U.S. polar icebreaking fleet consists of one heavy polar icebreaker (*Polar Star*) and one medium polar icebreaker (*Healy*). The new polar icebreaker for which initial acquisition funding is requested in the FY2013 budget would replace *Polar Star* at about the time *Polar Star's* 7- to 10-year reactivation period ends.

The Coast Guard's strategy document for the Arctic region, released on May 21, 2013, states that "The United States must have adequate icebreaking capability to support research that advances fundamental understanding of the region and its evolution," and that "The Nation must also make a strategic investment in icebreaking capability to enable access to the high latitudes over the long-term."

Potential issues for Congress regarding Coast Guard polar icebreaker modernization include the following:

- the time line for acquiring a new polar icebreaker, which appears to have become less certain in the FY2015 budget submission;

- the numbers and capabilities of polar icebreakers the Coast Guard will need in the future;

- the disposition of *Polar Sea*;

- whether the new polar icebreaker initiated in the FY2013 budget should be funded with incremental funding (as proposed in the Coast Guard's Five Year Capital Investment Plan) or full funding in a single year, as normally required under the executive branch's full funding policy;

- whether new polar icebreakers should be funded entirely in the Coast Guard budget, or partly or entirely in some other part of the federal budget, such as the

Department of Defense (DOD) budget, the National Science Foundation (NSF) budget, or both;

- whether to provide future icebreaking capability through construction of new ships or service life extensions of existing polar icebreakers; and

- whether future polar icebreakers should be acquired through a traditional acquisition or a leasing arrangement.

Contents

Figures

Tables

Contacts

Introduction

This report provides background information and issues for Congress on the sustainment and modernization of the Coast Guard's polar icebreaker fleet, which performs a variety of missions supporting U.S. interests in polar regions. The Coast Guard's proposed FY2015 budget requests $6 million to continue initial acquisition activities for a new polar icebreaker.

The issue for Congress is whether to approve, reject, or modify Coast Guard plans for sustaining and modernizing its polar icebreaking fleet. Congressional decisions on this issue could affect Coast Guard funding requirements, the Coast Guard's ability to perform its polar missions, and the U.S. shipbuilding industrial base.

Background

Missions of U.S. Polar Icebreakers

The missions of U.S. polar icebreakers can be summarized as follows:

- conducting and supporting scientific research in the Arctic and Antarctic;

- defending U.S. sovereignty in the Arctic by helping to maintain a U.S. presence in U.S. territorial waters in the region;

- defending other U.S. interests in polar regions, including economic interests in waters that are within the U.S. exclusive economic zone (EEZ) north of Alaska;

- monitoring sea traffic in the Arctic, including ships bound for the United States; and

- conducting other typical Coast Guard missions (such as search and rescue, law enforcement, and protection of marine resources) in Arctic waters, including U.S. territorial waters north of Alaska.

Operations to support National Science Foundation (NSF) research activities in the Arctic and Antarctic have accounted in the past for a significant portion of U.S. polar icebreaker operations.[1] Supporting NSF research in the Antarctic has included performing an annual mission, called Operation Deep Freeze, to break through the Antarctic ice so as to resupply McMurdo Station, the large U.S. Antarctic research station located on the shore of McMurdo Sound, near the Ross Ice Shelf.

Although polar ice is diminishing due to climate change, observers generally expect that this development will not eliminate the need for U.S. polar icebreakers, and in some respects might increase mission demands for them. Even with the diminishment of polar ice, there are still significant ice-covered areas in the polar regions. Diminishment of polar ice could lead in coming

---

[1] This passage, beginning with "The missions of...", originated in an earlier iteration of this CRS report and was later transferred by GAO with minor changes to Government Accountability Office, *Coast Guard[:]Efforts to Identify Arctic Requirements Are Ongoing, but More Communication about Agency Planning Efforts Would Be Beneficial*, GAO-10-870, September 2010, p. 53.

years to increased commercial ship, cruise ship, and naval surface ship operations, as well as increased exploration for oil and other resources, in the Arctic—activities that could require increased levels of support from polar icebreakers.[2] Changing ice conditions in Antarctic waters have made the McMurdo resupply mission more challenging since 2000.[3] An April 18, 2011, press report states that the Commandant of the Coast Guard at the time, Admiral Robert Papp,

> sees plenty of reasons the United States will need polar icebreakers for the "foreseeable future," despite speculation that thinning ice in the Arctic could make the icebreakers replaceable with other ice-hardened ships, the admiral said last week....
>
> "I don't see that causing us to back down on some minimal level of polar icebreakers," Papp told *Inside the Navy*. "The fact of the matter is, there's still winter ice that's forming [each year]. It's coming down pretty far. We don't need to get up there just during summer months when there's open water."[4]

The Coast Guard's strategy document for the Arctic region, released on May 21, 2013, states that "The United States must have adequate icebreaking capability to support research that advances fundamental understanding of the region and its evolution," and that "The Nation must also make a strategic investment in icebreaking capability to enable access to the high latitudes over the long-term."[5]

Current U.S. Polar Icebreakers

The U.S. polar icebreaker fleet currently includes four ships—three Coast Guard ships and one ship operated by the NSF. The ships are described briefly below.

Three Coast Guard Ships

The Coast Guard's three polar icebreakers are multimission ships that can break through ice, support scientific research operations, and perform other missions typically performed by Coast Guard ships.

Heavy Polar Icebreakers Polar Star and Polar Sea

Polar Star (WAGB-10) and *Polar Sea* (WAGB-11),[6] sister ships built to the same general design (**Figure 1** and **Figure 2**), were procured in the early 1970s as replacements for earlier U.S. icebreakers. They were designed for 30-year service lives, and were built by Lockheed

---

[2] For more on changes in the Arctic due to diminishment of Arctic ice, see CRS Report R41153, *Changes in the Arctic: Background and Issues for Congress*, coordinated by Ronald O'Rourke.

[3] National Research Council, *Polar Icebreakers in a Changing World, An Assessment of U.S. Needs*, Washington, 2007, pp. 6-7, 14, 63.

[4] Cid Standifer, "Adm. Papp: Coast Guard Still Needs Icebreakers For Winter, Antarctic," *Inside the Navy*, April 18, 2011.

[5] *United States Coast Guard Arctic Strategy*, Washington, May 2013, p. 35; accessed May 24, 2013, at http://www.uscg mil/seniorleadership/DOCS/CG_Arctic_Strategy.pdf.

[6] The designation WAGB means Coast Guard icebreaker. More specifically, W means Coast Guard ship, A means auxiliary, G means miscellaneous purpose, and B means icebreaker.

Shipbuilding of Seattle, WA, a division of Lockheed that also built ships for the U.S. Navy, but which exited the shipbuilding business in the late 1980s.

The ships are 399 feet long and displace about 13,200 tons.[7] They are among the world's most powerful non-nuclear-powered icebreakers, with a capability to break through ice up to 6 feet thick at a speed of 3 knots. Because of their icebreaking capability, they are considered heavy polar icebreakers. In addition to a crew of 134, each ship can embark a scientific research staff of 32 people.

Figure 1. *Polar Star* and *Polar Sea*

(Side by side in McMurdo Sound, Antarctica)

Source: Coast Guard photo accessed at http://www.uscg.mil/pacarea/cgcpolarsea/history.asp on April 21, 2011.

Polar Star was commissioned into service on January 19, 1976, and consequently is now several years beyond its intended 30-year service life. Due to worn out electric motors and other problems, the Coast Guard placed the ship in caretaker status on July 1, 2006.[8] Congress in FY2009 and FY2010 provided funding to repair *Polar Star* and return it to service for 7 to 10 years; the repair work, which reportedly cost about $57 million, was completed, and the ship was

---

[7] By comparison, the Coast Guard's new National Security Cutters—its new high-endurance cutters—are about 418 feet long and displace roughly 4,000 tons.

[8] Source for July 1, 2006, date: U.S. Coast Guard email to CRS on February 22, 2008. The Coast Guard's official term for caretaker status is "In Commission, Special."

reactivated on December 14, 2012.[9] The ship completed ice trials in the Arctic in June and July of 2013, was certified as mission ready in November 2013, and departed Seattle in December 2013 for deployment to Antarctica at the request of the NSF in support of the annual McMurdo resupply operation (aka Operation Deep Freeze).[10] Although the repair work on the ship was intended to give it another 7 to 10 years of service, an August 30, 2010, press report quoted then-Commandant of the Coast Guard, Admiral Robert Papp, as saying, "We're getting her back into service, but it's a little uncertain to me how many more years we can get out of her in her current condition, even after we do the engine repairs."[11]

Figure 2. *Polar Sea*

Source: Coast Guard photo accessed at http://www.uscg.mil/pacarea/cgcpolarsea/img/PSEApics/FullShip2.jpg on April 21, 2011.

Polar Sea was commissioned into service on February 23, 1978, and consequently is also beyond its originally intended 30-year service life. In 2006, the Coast Guard completed a rehabilitation project that extended the ship's expected service life to 2014. On June 25, 2010, however, the Coast Guard announced that *Polar Sea* had suffered an unexpected engine casualty, and the ship was unavailable for operation after that.[12] The Coast Guard placed *Polar Sea* in commissioned,

---

[9] See, for example, Kyung M. Song, "Icebreaker Polar Star Gets $57 Million Overhaul," *Seattle Times*, December 14, 2012.

[10] Source: Email to CRS from Coast Guard Mobility and Ice Operations Division, April 16, 2014.

[11] Cid Standifer, "Papp: Refurbished Icebreaker Hulls Could Last 'An Awful Long Time,'" *Inside the Navy*, August 30, 2010.

[12] On June 25, 2010, the Coast Guard announced that

> POLAR SEA suffered an unexpected engine casualty and will be unable to deploy on its scheduled fall 2010 Arctic patrol and may be unavailable for Operation Deep Freeze [the annual mission to break through the Antarctic ice so as to resupply McMurdo Station], Dec. 20 to Jan 2, 2011.
>
> POLAR SEA will likely be in a maintenance status and unavailable for operation until at least January 2011....
>
> Currently, the 420-foot CGC HEALY, commissioned in 1999, is the service's sole operational polar region icebreaker. While the HEALY is capable of supporting a wide range of Coast Guard missions in the polar regions, it is a medium icebreaker capable of breaking ice up to 4.5-feet thick

(continued...)

---

inactive status on October 14, 2011. The Coast Guard transferred certain major equipment from *Polar Sea* to *Polar Star* to facilitate *Polar Star*'s return to service.[13]

Section 222 of the Coast Guard and Maritime Transportation Act of 2012 (H.R. 2838/P.L. 112-213 of December 20, 2012) prohibited the Coast Guard from removing any part of *Polar Sea* and from transferring, relinquishing ownership of, dismantling, or recycling the ship until it submitteds a business case analysis of the options for and costs of reactivating the ship and extending its service life to at least September 30, 2022, so as to maintain U.S. polar icebreaking capabilities and fulfill the Coast Guard's high latitude mission needs, as identified in the Coast Guard's July 2010 High Latitude Study. (The business case analysis was submitted to Congress with a cover date of November 7, 2013.)

Medium Polar Icebreaker Healy

Healy (WAGB-20) (**Figure 3**) was procured in the early 1990s as a complement to *Polar Star* and *Polar Sea*, and was commissioned into service on August 21, 2000. The ship was built by Avondale Industries, a shipyard located near New Orleans, LA, that built numerous Coast Guard and Navy ships, and which now forms part of Huntington Ingalls Industries (HII).[14]

Healy is a bit larger than *Polar Star* and *Polar Sea*—it is 420 feet long and displaces about 16,000 tons. Compared to *Polar Star* and *Polar Sea*, *Healy* has less icebreaking capability (it is considered a medium polar icebreaker), but more capability for supporting scientific research. The ship can break through ice up to 4½ feet thick at a speed of 3 knots, and embark a scientific research staff of 35 (with room for another 15 surge personnel and 2 visitors). The ship is used primarily for supporting scientific research in the Arctic.

(...continued)

> at three knots.

> The impact on POLAR SEA's scheduled 2011 Arctic winter science deployment, scheduled for Jan. 3 to Feb. 23, 2011, is not yet known and depends on the scope of required engine repair.

> ("Icebreaker POLAR SEA Sidelined By Engine Troubles," *Coast Guard Compass (Official Blog of the U.S. Coast Guard)*, June 25, 2010.)

A June 25, 2010, report stated that "inspections of the Polar Sea's main diesel engines revealed excessive wear in 33 cylinder assemblies. The Coast Guard is investigating the root cause and hopes to have an answer by August." ("USCG Cancels Polar Icebreaker's Fall Deployment," *DefenseNews.com*, June 25, 2010.) Another June 25 report stated that "five of [the ship's] six mighty engines are stilled, some with worn pistons essentially welded to their sleeves." (Andrew C. Revkin, "America's Heavy Icebreakers Are Both Broken Down," *Dot Earth (New York Times blog)*, June 25, 2010.)

[13] Source: October 17, 2011, email to CRS from Coast Guard Congressional Affairs office.

[14] HII was previously owned by Northrop Grumman, during which time it was known as Northrop Grumman Shipbuilding.

Figure 3. *Healy*

Source: Coast Guard photo accessed at http://www.uscg.mil/history/webcutters/Healy_CGC_1_300.jpg on April 21, 2011.

One National Science Foundation Ship

The nation's fourth polar icebreaker is *Nathaniel B. Palmer*, which was built for the NSF in 1992 by North American Shipbuilding, of Larose, LA. The ship, called *Palmer* for short, is owned by Offshore Service Vessels LLC, operated by Edison Chouest Offshore (ECO) of Galliano, LA (a firm that owns and operates research ships and offshore deepwater service ships),[15] and chartered by the NSF. *Palmer* is considerably smaller than the Coast Guard's three polar icebreakers—it is 308 feet long and has a displacement of about 6,500 tons. It is operated by a crew of about 22, and can embark a scientific staff of 27 to 37.[16]

Unlike the Coast Guard's three polar icebreakers, which are multimission ships, *Palmer* was purpose-built as a single-mission ship for conducting and supporting scientific research in the Antarctic. It has less icebreaking capability than the Coast Guard's polar icebreakers, being capable of breaking ice up to 3 feet thick at speeds of 3 knots. This capability is sufficient for breaking through the more benign ice conditions found in the vicinity of the Antarctic Peninsula,

---

[15] For more on ECO, see the firm's website at http://www.chouest.com/.

[16] Sources vary on the exact number of scientific staff that can be embarked on *Palmer*. For some basic information on the ship, see http://www.nsf.gov/od/opp/support/nathpalm.jsp,

http://www.usap.gov/vesselScienceAndOperations/documents/prvnews_june03.pdfprvnews_june03.pdf,

http://nsf.gov/od/opp/antarct/treaty/pdf/plans0607/15plan07.pdf,

http://www.nsf.gov/pubs/1996/nsf9693/fls htm, and

http://www.hazegray.org/worldnav/usa/nsf htm.

so as to resupply Palmer Station, a U.S. research station on the peninsula. Some observers might view *Palmer* not so much as an icebreaker as an oceanographic research ship with enough icebreaking capability for the Antarctic Peninsula. *Palmer's* icebreaking capability is not considered sufficient to perform the McMurdo resupply mission.

Summary

In summary, the U.S. polar icebreaking fleet currently includes

- two heavy polar icebreakers (*Polar Star* and *Polar Sea*), one of which is operational, that are designed to perform missions in either polar area, including the challenging McMurdo resupply mission;

- one medium polar icebreaker (*Healy*) that is used primarily for scientific research in the Arctic; and

- one ship (*Palmer*) that is used for scientific research in the Antarctic.

Table 1 summarizes the four ships.

Table 1. U.S. Polar Icebreakers

	Polar Star	Polar Sea	Healy	Palmer
Operator	USCG	USCG	USCG	NSF
U.S.-Government owned?	Yes	Yes	Yes	No[a]
Currently operational?	Yes (reactivated on December 14, 2012)	No	Yes	Yes
Entered service	1976	1978	2000	1992
Length (feet)	399	399	420	308
Displacement (tons)	13,200	13,200	16,000	6,500
Icebreaking capability at 3 knots (ice thickness in feet)	6 feet	6 feet	4.5 feet	3 feet
Ice ramming capability (ice thickness in feet)	21 feet	21 feet	8 feet	n/a
Operating temperature	-60° Fahrenheit	-60° Fahrenheit	-50° Fahrenheit	n/a
Crew (when operational)	155[b]	155[b]	85[c]	22
Additional scientific staff	32	32	35[d]	27-37

Sources: Prepared by CRS using data from U.S. Coast Guard, National Research Council, National Science Foundation, Department of Homeland Security (DHS) Office of Inspector General, and (for *Palmer*) additional online reference sources. n/a is not available.

a. Owned by Edison Chouest Offshore (ECO) of Galliano, LA, and leased to NSF through Raytheon Polar Services Company (RPSC).

b. Includes 24 officers, 20 chief petty officers, 102 enlisted, and 9 in the aviation detachment.

c. Includes 19 officers, 12 chief petty officers, and 54 enlisted.

d. In addition to 85 crew members 85 and 35 scientists, the ship can accommodate another 15 surge personnel and 2 visitors.

In addition to the four ships shown in **Table 1**, a fifth U.S.-registered polar ship with icebreaking capability—the icebreaking anchor handling tug supply vessel *Aiviq*—is used by Royal Dutch Shell oil company to support oil exploration and drilling in Arctic waters off Alaska. The ship, which completed construction in 2012, is owned ECO and chartered by Royal Dutch Shell. It is used primarily for towing and laying anchors for drilling rigs, but is also equipped for responding to oil spills.

January 2014 Implementation Plan for National Strategy for Arctic Region

On May 10, 2013, the Obama Administration released a document entitled *National Strategy for the Arctic Region*.[17] On January 30, 2014, the Obama Administration released an implementation plan for this strategy.[18] Of the 36 or so specific initiatives in the implementation plan, one is entitled "Sustain federal capability to conduct maritime operations in ice-impacted waters." The implementation plan states the following regarding this initiative:

> *Objective:* Ensure the United States maintains icebreaking and ice-strengthened ship capability with sufficient capacity to project a sovereign U.S. maritime presence, support U.S. interests in the Polar Regions and facilitate research that advances the fundamental understanding of the Arctic.
>
> *Next Steps:* The Federal Government requires the ability to conduct operations in ice-impacted waters in the Arctic. As maritime activity in the Arctic region increases, expanded access will be required. Next steps include:
>
> • The lead and supporting Departments and Agencies will develop a document that lists the capabilities needed to operate in ice-impacted waters to support Federal activities in the Polar Regions and emergent sovereign responsibilities over the next ten to twenty years by the end of 2014.
>
> • Develop long-term plans to sustain Federal capability to physically access the Arctic with sufficient capacity to support U.S. interests by the end of 2017.
>
> *Measuring Progress:* Sustaining federal capability will be demonstrated through the Federal Government's ability to conduct operations in the Arctic to support statutory missions and sovereign responsibilities, and to advance interests in the region. Progress in implementing this objective will be measured by completion of the capabilities document, and long term sustainment plan.
>
> *Lead Agency:* Department of Homeland Security
>
> *Supporting Agencies:* Department of Commerce (National Oceanic and Atmospheric Administration), Department of Defense, Department of State, Department of Transportation, National Science Foundation[.][19]

---

[17] *National Strategy for the Arctic Region*, May 2013, 11 pp.; accessed May 14, 2013, at http://www.whitehouse.gov/ sites/default/files/docs/nat_arctic_strategy.pdf. The document includes a cover letter from President Obama dated May 10, 2013.

[18] The White House new release about the release of the implementation plan was posted at http://www.whitehouse.gov/blog/2014/01/30/white-house-releases-implementation-plan-national-strategy-arctic-region. The document is posted at http://www.whitehouse.gov/sites/default/files/docs/ implementation_plan_for_the_national_strategy_for_the_arctic_region_-_fi....pdf.

[19] *Implementation Plan for The National Strategy for the Arctic Region*, January 2014, pp. 8-9.

Recent Studies Relating to Coast Guard Polar Icebreakers

A number of studies have been conducted in recent years to assess U.S. requirements for polar icebreakers and options for sustaining and modernizing the Coast Guard's polar icebreaker fleet. This section presents the findings of some of these studies.

Coast Guard High Latitude Study Provided to Congress in July 2011

In July 2011, the Coast Guard provided to Congress a study on the Coast Guard's missions and capabilities for operations in high-latitude (i.e., polar) areas. The study, commonly known as the High Latitude Study, is dated July 2010 on its cover. The High Latitude Study concluded the following:

> [The study] concludes that future capability and capacity gaps will significantly impact four [Coast Guard] mission areas in the Arctic: Defense Readiness, Ice Operations, Marine Environmental Protection, and Ports, Waterways, and Coastal Security. These mission areas address the protection of important national interests in a geographic area where other nations are actively pursuing their own national goals....

> The common and dominant contributor to these significant mission impacts is the gap in polar icebreaking capability. The increasing obsolescence of the Coast Guard's icebreaker fleet will further exacerbate mission performance gaps in the coming years....

> The gap in polar icebreaking capacity has resulted in a lack of at-sea time for crews and senior personnel and a corresponding gap in training and leadership. In addition to providing multi-mission capability and intrinsic mobility, a helicopter-capable surface unit would eliminate the need for acquiring an expensive shore-based infrastructure that may only be needed on a seasonal or occasional basis. The most capable surface unit would be a polar icebreaker. Polar icebreakers can transit safely in a variety of ice conditions and have the endurance to operate far from logistics bases. The Coast Guard's polar icebreakers have conducted a wide range of planned and unscheduled Coast Guard missions in the past. Polar icebreakers possess the ability to carry large numbers of passengers, cargo, boats, and helicopters. Polar icebreakers also have substantial command, control, and communications capabilities. The flexibility and mobility of polar icebreakers would assist the Coast Guard in closing future mission performance gaps effectively....

> Existing capability and capacity gaps are expected to significantly impact future Coast Guard performance in two Antarctic mission areas: Defense Readiness and Ice Operations. Future gaps may involve an inability to carry out probable and easily projected mission requirements, such as the McMurdo resupply, or readiness to respond to less-predictable events. By their nature, contingencies requiring the use of military capabilities often occur quickly. As is the case in the Arctic, the deterioration of the Coast Guard's icebreaker fleet is the primary driver for this significant mission impact. This will further widen mission performance gaps in the coming years. The recently issued Naval Operations Concept 2010 requires a surface presence in both the Arctic and Antarctic. This further exacerbates the capability gap left by the deterioration of the icebreaker fleet....

> The significant deterioration of the Coast Guard icebreaker fleet and the emerging mission demands to meet future functional requirements in the high latitude regions dictate that the Coast Guard acquire material solutions to close the capability gaps....

> To meet the Coast Guard mission functional requirement, the Coast Guard icebreaking fleet must be capable of supporting the following missions:

- **Arctic North Patrol.** Continuous multimission icebreaker presence in the Arctic.

- **Arctic West Science.** Spring and summer science support in the Arctic.

- **Antarctic, McMurdo Station resupply.** Planned deployment for break-in, supply ship escort, and science support. This mission, conducted in the Antarctic summer, also requires standby icebreaker support for backup in the event the primary vessel cannot complete the mission.

- **Thule Air Base Resupply and Polar Region Freedom of Navigation Transits.** Provide vessel escort operations in support of the Military Sealift Command's Operation Pacer Goose; then complete any Freedom of Navigation exercises in the region.

In addition, the joint Naval Operations Concept establishes the following mission requirements:

- **Assured access and assertion of U.S. policy in the Polar Regions.** The current demand for this mission requires continuous icebreaker presence in both Polar Regions.

Considering these missions, the analysis yields the following findings:

- **The Coast Guard requires three heavy and three medium icebreakers to fulfill its statutory missions.** These icebreakers are necessary to (1) satisfy Arctic winter and transition season demands and (2) provide sufficient capacity to also execute summer missions. Single-crewed icebreakers have sufficient capacity for all current and expected statutory missions. Multiple crewing provides no advantage because the number of icebreakers required is driven by winter and shoulder season requirements. Future use of multiple or augmented crews could provide additional capacity needed to absorb mission growth.

- **The Coast Guard requires six heavy and four medium icebreakers to fulfill its statutory missions and maintain the continuous presence requirements of the Naval Operations Concept.** Consistent with current practice, these icebreakers are single-crewed and homeported in Seattle Washington.

- **Applying crewing and home porting alternatives reduces the overall requirement to four heavy and two medium icebreakers.** This assessment of non-material solutions shows that the reduced number of icebreakers can be achieved by having all vessels operate with multiple crews and two of the heavy icebreakers homeporting in the Southern Hemisphere.

Leasing was also considered as a nonmaterial solution. While there is no dispute that the Coast Guard's polar icebreaker fleet is in need of recapitalization, the decision to acquire this capability through purchase of new vessels, reconstruction of existing ships, or commercial lease of suitable vessels must be resolved to provide the best value to the taxpayer. The multi-mission nature of the Coast Guard may provide opportunities to conduct some subset of its missions with non government-owned vessels. However, serious consideration must be given to the fact that the inherently governmental missions of the Coast Guard must be performed using government-owned and operated vessels. An interpretation of the national policy is needed to determine the resource level that best supports the nation's interests....

The existing icebreaker capacity, two inoperative heavy icebreakers and an operational medium icebreaker, does not represent a viable capability to the federal government. The time needed to augment this capability is on the order of 10 years. At that point, around 2020, the heavy icebreaking capability bridging strategy expires.[20]

At a July 27, 2011, hearing on U.S. economic interests in the Arctic before the Oceans, Atmosphere, Fisheries, and Coast Guard subcommittee of the Senate Commerce, Science, and Transportation Committee, the following exchange occurred:

> SENATOR OLYMPIA J. SNOWE: On the high latitude study, do you agree with—and those—I would like to also hear from you, Admiral Titley, as well, on these requirements in terms of Coast Guard vessels as I understand it, they want to have—I guess, it was a three medium ice breakers. Am in correct in saying that? Three medium ice breakers.
>
> ADMIRAL ROBERT PAPP, COMMANDANT OF THE COAST GUARD: I agree with the mission analysis and as you look at the requirements for the things that we might do up there, if it is in the nation's interest, it identifies a minimum requirement for three heavy ice breakers and three medium ice breakers and then if you want a persistent presence up there, it would require—and also doing things such as breaking out (inaudible) and other responsibilities, then it would take up to a maximum six heavy and four medium.
>
> SNOWE: Right. Do you agree with that?
>
> PAPP: If we were to be charged with carrying out those full responsibilities, yes, ma'am. Those are the numbers that you would need to do it.
>
> SNOWE: Admiral Titley, how would you respond to the high latitude study and has the Navy conducted its own assessment of its capability?
>
> REAR ADMIRAL DAVID TITLEY, OCEANORGRAPHER AND NAVIGATOR OF THE NAVY: Ma'am, we are in the process right now of conducting what we call a capabilities based assessment that will be out in the summer of this year.
>
> We are getting ready to finish that—the Coast Guard has been a key component of the Navy's task force on climate change, literally since day one when the Chief of Naval Operations set this up, that morning, we had the Coast Guard invited as a member of our executive steering committee.
>
> So we have been working very closely with the Coast Guard, with the Department of Homeland Security, and I think Admiral Papp—said it best as far as the specific comments on the high latitude study but we have been working very closely with the Coast Guard.[21]

January 2011 DHS Office of Inspector General Report

A January 2011 report on the Coast Guard's polar icebreakers from Department of Homeland Security (DHS) Office of the Inspector General stated:

> The Coast Guard does not have the necessary budgetary control over its [polar] icebreakers, nor does it have a sufficient number of icebreakers to accomplish its missions in the Polar Regions. Currently, the Coast Guard has only one operational [polar] icebreaker [i.e., *Healy*], making it necessary for the United States to contract with foreign nations to perform

---

[20] *United States Coast Guard High Latitude Region Mission Analysis Capstone Summary*, July 2010, pp. 10-13, 15.

[21] Source: Transcript of hearing.

scientific, logistical, and supply activities. Without the necessary budgetary control and a sufficient number of icebreaking assets, the Coast Guard will not have the capability to perform all of its missions, will lose critical icebreaking expertise, and may be beholden to foreign nations to perform its statutory missions. The Coast Guard should improve its strategic approach to ensure that it has the long-term icebreaker capabilities needed to support Coast Guard missions and other national interests in the Arctic and Antarctic regions.[22]

Regarding current polar icebreaking capabilities for performing Arctic missions, the report states:

The Coast Guard's icebreaking resources are unlikely to meet future demands. [The table below] outlines the missions that Coast Guard is unable to meet in the Arctic with its current icebreaking resources.

Arctic Missions Not Being Met

Requesting Agency	Missions Not Being Met
United States Coast Guard	—Fisheries enforcement in Bering Sea to prevent foreign fishing in U.S. waters and overfishing
	—Capability to conduct search and rescue in Beaufort Sea for cruise line and natural resource exploration ships
	—Future missions not anticipated to be met: 2010 Arctic Winter Science Deployment
NASA	Winter access to the Arctic to conduct oceanography and study Arctic currents and how they relate to regional ice cover, climate, and biology
NOAA and NSF	Winter research
Department of Defense	Assured access to ice-impacted waters through a persistent icebreaker presence in the Arctic and Antarctic[23]

The report also states:

Should the Coast Guard not obtain funding for new icebreakers or major service life extensions for its existing icebreakers with sufficient lead-time, the United States will have no heavy icebreaking capability beyond 2020 and no polar icebreaking capability of any kind by 2029. Without the continued use of icebreakers, the United States will lose its ability to maintain a presence in the Polar Regions, the Coast Guard's expertise to perform ice operations will continue to diminish, and missions will continue to go unmet.[24]

---

[22] Department of Homeland Security, Office of Inspector General, *The Coast Guard's Polar Icebreaker Maintenance, Upgrade, and Acquisition Program*, OIG-11-31, January 2011, p. 1 (Executive Summary). Report accessed September 21, 2011, at http://www.dhs.gov/xoig/assets/mgmtrpts/OIG_11-31_Jan11.pdf.

[23] Department of Homeland Security, Office of Inspector General, *The Coast Guard's Polar Icebreaker Maintenance, Upgrade, and Acquisition Program*, OIG-11-31, January 2011, p. 9.

[24] Department of Homeland Security, Office of Inspector General, *The Coast Guard's Polar Icebreaker Maintenance,* (continued...)

Regarding current polar icebreaking capabilities for performing Antarctic missions, the report states:

> The Coast Guard needs additional icebreakers to accomplish its missions in the Antarctic. The Coast Guard has performed the McMurdo Station resupply in Antarctica for decades, but with increasing difficulty in recent years. The Coast Guard's two heavy-duty icebreakers [i.e., *Polar Star* and *Polar Sea*] are at the end of their service lives, and have become less reliable and increasingly costly to keep in service....
>
> In recent years, the Coast Guard has found that ice conditions in the Antarctic have become more challenging for the resupply of McMurdo Station. The extreme ice conditions have necessitated the use of foreign vessels to perform the McMurdo break-in....
>
> As ice conditions continue to change around the Antarctic, two icebreakers are needed for the McMurdo break-in and resupply mission. Typically, one icebreaker performs the break-in and the other remains on standby. Should the first ship become stuck in the ice or should the ice be too thick for one icebreaker to complete the mission, the Coast Guard deploys the ship on standby. Since the Polar Sea and Polar Star are not currently in service, the Coast Guard has no icebreakers capable of performing this mission. [The table below] outlines the missions that will not be met without operational heavy-duty icebreakers.

Arctic Missions Not Being Met

Requesting Agency	Missions Not Being Met
NSF	Missions not anticipated to be met: 2010-2011 Operation Deep Freeze – McMurdo Station Resupply
Department of State	Additional inspections of foreign facilities in Antarctica to enforce the Antarctic Treaty and ensure facilities' environment compliance[25]

The report's conclusion and recommendations were as follows:

Conclusion

With an aging fleet of three icebreakers, one operational and two beyond their intended 30-year service life, the Coast Guard is at a critical crossroads in its Polar Icebreaker Maintenance, Upgrade, and Acquisition Program. It must clarify its mission requirements, and if the current mission requirements remain, the Coast Guard must determine the best method for meeting these requirements in the short and long term.

Recommendations

We recommend that the Assistant Commandant for Marine Safety, Security, and Stewardship:

(...continued)

Upgrade, and Acquisition Program, OIG-11-31, January 2011, p. 10.

[25] Department of Homeland Security, Office of Inspector General, *The Coast Guard's Polar Icebreaker Maintenance, Upgrade, and Acquisition Program*, OIG-11-31, January 2011, pp. 10-11.

Recommendation #1: Request budgetary authority for the operation, maintenance, and upgrade of its icebreakers.

Recommendation #2: In coordination with the Department of Homeland Security, request clarification from Congress to determine whether Arctic missions should be performed by Coast Guard assets or contracted vessels.

Recommendation #3: In coordination with the Department of Homeland Security, request clarification from Congress to determine whether Antarctic missions should be performed by Coast Guard assets or contracted vessels.

Recommendation #4: Conduct the necessary analysis to determine whether the Coast Guard should replace or perform service-life extensions on its two existing heavy-duty icebreaking ships.

Recommendation #5: Request appropriations necessary to meet mission requirements in the Arctic and Antarctic.[26]

The report states that

> The Coast Guard concurred with all five of the recommendations and is initiating corrective actions. We consider the recommendations open and unresolved. The Coast Guard provided information on some of its ongoing projects that will address the program needs identified in the report.[27]

2010 U.S. Arctic Research Commission Report

A May 2010 report from the U.S. Arctic Research Commission (USARC) on goals and objectives for Arctic research for 2009-2010 stated:

> To have an effective Arctic research program, the United States must invest in human capital, research platforms, and infrastructure, including new polar class icebreakers, and sustained sea, air, land, space, and social observing systems…. The Commission urges the President and Congress to commit to replacing the nation's two polar class icebreakers.[28]

2007 National Research Council Report

A 2007 National Research Council (NRC) report, *Polar Icebreakers in a Changing World: An Assessment of U.S. Needs*, assessed roles and future needs for Coast Guard polar icebreakers.[29] The study was required by report language accompanying the FY2005 DHS appropriations act (H.R. 4567/P.L. 108-334).[30] The study was completed in 2006 and published in 2007. Some

---

[26] Department of Homeland Security, Office of Inspector General, *The Coast Guard's Polar Icebreaker Maintenance, Upgrade, and Acquisition Program*, OIG-11-31, January 2011, p. 12.

[27] Department of Homeland Security, Office of Inspector General, *The Coast Guard's Polar Icebreaker Maintenance, Upgrade, and Acquisition Program*, OIG-11-31, January 2011, p. 13.

[28] U.S. Arctic Research Commission, *Report on Goals and Objectives for Arctic Research 2009–2010*, May 2010, p. 4. Accessed online December 5, 2011, at http://www.arctic.gov/publications/usarc_2009-10_goals.pdf.

[29] National Research Council, *Polar Icebreakers in a Changing World, An Assessment of U.S. Needs*, Washington, 2007, 122 pp.

[30] H.R. 4567/P.L. 108-334 of October 18, 2004. The related Senate bill was S. 2537. The Senate report on S. 2537 (continued...)

---

sources refer to the study as the 2006 NRC report. The report made the following conclusions and recommendations:

> Based on the current and future needs for icebreaking capabilities, the [study] committee concludes that the nation continues to require a polar icebreaking fleet that includes a minimum of three multimission ships [like the Coast Guard's three current polar icebreakers] and one single-mission [research] ship [like Palmer]. The committee finds that although the demand for icebreaking capability is predicted to increase, a fleet of three multimission and one single-mission icebreakers can meet the nation's future polar icebreaking needs through the application of the latest technology, creative crewing models, wise management of ice conditions, and more efficient use of the icebreaker fleet and other assets. The nation should immediately begin to program, design, and construct two new polar icebreakers to replace the POLAR STAR and POLAR SEA.
>
> Building only one new polar icebreaker is insufficient for several reasons. First, a single ship cannot be in more than one location at a time. No matter how technologically advanced or efficiently operated, a single polar icebreaker can operate in the polar regions for only a portion of any year. An icebreaker requires regular maintenance and technical support from shipyards and industrial facilities, must reprovision regularly, and has to effect periodic crew changeouts. A single icebreaker, therefore, could not meet any reasonable standard of active and influential presence and reliable, at-will access throughout the polar regions.
>
> A second consideration is the potential risk of failure in the harsh conditions of polar operations. Despite their intrinsic robustness, damage and system failure are always a risk and the U.S. fleet must have enough depth to provide backup assistance. Having only a single icebreaker would necessarily require the ship to accept a more conservative operating profile, avoiding more challenging ice conditions because reliable assistance would not be available. A second capable icebreaker, either operating elsewhere or in homeport, would provide ensured backup assistance and allow for more robust operations by the other ship.
>
> From a strategic, longer-term perspective, two new Polar class icebreakers will far better position the nation for the increasing challenges emerging in both polar regions. A second new ship would allow the U.S. Coast Guard to reestablish an active patrol presence in U.S.

(...continued)

(S.Rept. 108-280 of June 17, 2004) stated:

> The Committee expects the Commandant to enter into an arrangement with the National Academy of Sciences to conduct a comprehensive study of the role of Coast Guard icebreakers in supporting United States operations in the Antarctic and the Arctic. The study should include different scenarios for continuing those operations including service life extension or replacement of existing Coast Guard icebreakers and alternative methods that do not use Coast Guard icebreakers. The study should also address changes in the roles and missions of Coast Guard icebreakers in support of future marine operations in the Arctic that may develop due to environmental change, including the amount and kind of icebreaking support that may be required in the future to support marine operations in the Northern Sea Route and the Northwest Passage; the suitability of the Polar Class icebreakers for these new roles; and appropriate changes in existing laws governing Coast Guard icebreaking operations and the potential for new operating regimes. The study should be submitted to the Committee no later than September 30, 2005.

The conference report on H.R. 4567 (H.Rept. 108-774 of October 9, 2004) stated:

> As discussed in the Senate report and the Coast Guard authorization bill for fiscal year 2005, the conferees require the National Academy of Sciences to study the role of Coast Guard icebreakers.

The earlier House report on H.R. 4567 (H.Rept. 108-541 of June 15, 2004) contained language directing a similar report from the Coast Guard rather than the National Academies. (See the passage in the House report under the header "Icebreaking.")

waters north of Alaska to meet statutory responsibilities that will inevitably derive from increased human activity, economic development, and environmental change. It would allow response to emergencies such as search-and-rescue cases, pollution incidents, and assistance to ships threatened with grounding or damage by ice. Moreover, a second new ship will leverage the possibilities for simultaneous operations in widely disparate geographic areas (e.g., concurrent operations in the Arctic and Antarctic), provide more flexibility for conducting Antarctic logistics (as either the primary or the secondary ship for the McMurdo break-in), allow safer multiple-ship operations in the most demanding ice conditions, and increase opportunities for international expeditions. Finally, an up-front decision to build two new polar icebreakers will allow economies in the design and construction process and provide a predictable cost reduction for the second ship....

The [study] committee finds that both operations and maintenance of the polar icebreaker fleet have been underfunded for many years, and the capabilities of the nation's icebreaking fleet have diminished substantially. Deferred long-term maintenance and failure to execute a plan for replacement or refurbishment of the nation's icebreaking ships have placed national interests in the polar regions at risk. The nation needs the capability to operate in both polar regions reliably and at will. Specifically, the committee recommends the following:

- The United States should continue to project an active and influential presence in the Arctic to support its interests. This requires U.S. government polar icebreaking capability to ensure year-round access throughout the region.

- The United States should continue to project an active and influential presence in the Antarctic to support its interests. The nation should reliably control sufficient icebreaking capability to break a channel into and ensure the maritime resupply of McMurdo Station.

- The United States should maintain leadership in polar research. This requires icebreaking capability to provide access to the deep Arctic and the ice-covered waters of the Antarctic.

- National interests in the polar regions require that the United States immediately program, budget, design, and construct two new polar icebreakers to be operated by the U.S. Coast Guard.

- To provide continuity of U.S. icebreaking capabilities, the POLAR SEA should remain mission capable and the POLAR STAR should remain available for reactivation until the new polar icebreakers enter service.

- The U.S. Coast Guard should be provided sufficient operations and maintenance budget to support an increased, regular, and influential presence in the Arctic. Other agencies should reimburse incremental costs associated with directed mission tasking.

- Polar icebreakers are essential instruments of U.S. national policy in the changing polar regions. To ensure adequate national icebreaking capability into the future, a Presidential Decision Directive should be issued to clearly align agency responsibilities and budgetary authorities.[31]

---

[31] National Research Council, *Polar Icebreakers in a Changing World, An Assessment of U.S. Needs*, Washington, 2007, pp. 2-3.

The Coast Guard stated in 2008 that it "generally supports" the NRC report, and that the Coast Guard "is working closely with interagency partners to determine a way forward with national polar policy that identifies broad U.S. interests and priorities in the Arctic and Antarctic that will ensure adequate maritime presence to further these interests. Identification and prioritization of U.S. national interests in these regions should drive development of associated USCG [U.S. Coast Guard] capability and resource requirements." The Coast Guard also stated: "Until those broad U.S. interests and priorities are identified, the current USG [U.S. Government] polar icebreaking fleet should be maintained in an operational status."[32]

Cost Estimates for Certain Modernization Options

New Replacement Ships

The Coast Guard estimated in February 2008 that new replacement ships for the *Polar Star* and *Polar Sea* might cost between $800 million and $925 million per ship in 2008 dollars to procure.[33] The Coast Guard said that this estimate

> is based on a ship with integrated electric drive, three propellers, and a combined diesel and gas (electric) propulsion plant. The icebreaking capability would be equivalent to the POLAR Class Icebreakers [i.e., Polar Star and Polar Sea] and research facilities and accommodations equivalent to HEALY. This cost includes all shipyard and government project costs. Total time to procure a new icebreaker [including mission analysis, studies, design, contract award, and construction] is eight to ten years.[34]

The Coast Guard further stated that this notional new ship would be designed for a 30-year service life.

The High Latitude Study provided to Congress in July 2011 states that the above figure of $800 million to $925 million in 2008 dollars equates to $900 million to $1,041 million in 2012 dollars. The study provides the following estimates, in 2012 dollars, of the acquisition costs for new polar icebreakers:

- $856 million for 1 ship;

- $1,663 million for 2 ships—an average of about $832 million each;

- $2,439 million for 3 ships—an average of $813 million each;

- $3,207 million for 4 ships—an average of about $802 million each;

---

[32] Coast Guard point paper provided to CRS on February 12, 2008, and dated with the same date, providing answers to questions from CRS concerning polar icebreaker modernization.

[33] Coast Guard point paper provided to CRS on February 12, 2008, and dated with the same date, providing answers to questions from CRS concerning polar icebreaker modernization.

[34] The Coast Guard states further that the estimate is based on the procurement cost of the *Mackinaw* (WAGB-30), a Great Lakes icebreaker that was procured a few years ago and commissioned into service with the Coast Guard in June 2006. The *Mackinaw* is 240 feet long, displaces 3,500 tons, and can break ice up to 2 feet, 8 inches thick at speeds of 3 knots, which is suitable for Great Lakes icebreaking. The Coast Guard says it scaled up the procurement cost for the *Mackinaw* in proportion to its size compared to that of a polar icebreaker, and then adjusted the resulting figure to account for the above-described capabilities of the notional replacement ship and recent construction costs at U.S. Gulf Coast shipyards.

- $3,961 million for 5 ships—an average of about $792 million each; and

- $4,704 million for 6 ships—an average of $784 million each.

The study refers to the above estimates as "rough order-of-magnitude costs" that "were developed as part of the Coast Guard's independent Polar Platform Business Case Analysis."[35]

25-Year Service Life Extensions

The Coast Guard stated in February 2008 that performing the extensive maintenance, repair, and modernization work needed to extend the service lives of the two ships by 25 years might cost roughly $400 million per ship. This figure, the Coast Guard said, is based on assessments made by independent contractors for the Coast Guard in 2004. The service life extension work, the Coast Guard said, would improve the two icebreakers' installed systems in certain areas. Although the work would be intended to permit the ships to operate for another 25 years, it would not return the cutters to new condition.[36]

An August 30, 2010, press report stated that the Commandant of the Coast Guard at the time, Admiral Robert Papp, estimated the cost of extending the lives of *Polar Star* and *Polar Sea* at about $500 million per ship; the article quoted Papp as stating that *Polar Star* and *Polar Sea* "were built to take a beating. They were built with very thick special steel, so you might be able to do a renovation on them and keep going.... I think there are certain types of steel that, if properly maintained, they can go on for an awful long time. What the limit is, I'm not sure."[37]

Reactivate *Polar Sea* for Several Years

At a June 26, 2013, hearing before the Coast Guard and Maritime Transportation subcommittee of the House Transportation and Infrastructure Committee, Vice Admiral John P. Currier, the Vice Commandant of the Coast Guard, testified that repairing and reactivating *Polar Sea* for an additional 7 to 10 years of service would require about 3 years of repair work at a cost of about $100 million.[38]

As mentioned earlier, the business case analysis required by Section 222 of H.R. 2838/P.L. 112-213 was submitted to Congress with a cover date of November 7, 2013. The executive summary of the analysis states:

> **Findings:**
>
> A total of 43 mission critical systems in five general categories were assessed and assigned a condition rating. Overall, Propulsion, Auxiliary and Prime Mission Equipment are rated Poor to Fair, while Structure and Habitability are rated Fair to Good. POLAR SEA reactivation is estimated to cost $99.2 million (excluding annual operations and support costs) to provide 7-10 years of service to the Coast Guard. Given the age of the icebreaker, operations and

---

[35] *United States Coast Guard High Latitude Region Mission Analysis Capstone Summary*, July 2010, p. 13.

[36] Coast Guard point paper provided to CRS on February 12, 2008, and dated with the same date, providing answers to questions from CRS concerning polar icebreaker modernization.

[37] Cid Standifer, "Papp: Refurbished Icebreaker Hulls Could Last 'An Awful Long Time,'" *Inside the Navy*, August 30, 2010. Ellipsis as in original.

[38] Transcript of hearing.

support costs are projected to rise from $36.6 million in the first year of operation to $52.8 million in the tenth year of operation. Combining reactivation costs and point estimates for operating costs, reactivation would cost $573.9 million. Accounting for operational and technical uncertainties, using a 90% Confidence Level Risk Analysis, the total potential cost rises to $751.7 million.

Arctic seasonal icebreaking demands through 2022 can be met with existing and planned Coast Guard assets, as current requirements do not justify the need for heavy icebreaking capability in the Arctic. Heavy icebreaker capability is needed to perform Operation Deep Freeze in Antarctica, but Coast Guard assets may not be the only option available to the National Science Foundation to support this activity. Although a second heavy icebreaker would provide redundancy, the cost of this redundant capability would come at the expense of more pressing and immediate operational demands. POLAR STAR, when fully reactivated, will provide heavy icebreaker capability until a new icebreaker can be delivered to meet both current and emerging requirements.[39]

Funding for New Polar Icebreaker

FY2013 Budget Submission

The Coast Guard's FY2013 budget initiated a new project for the design and construction of a new polar icebreaker. The Coast Guard's proposed FY2013 budget requested $8 million in FY2013 acquisition funding to initiate survey and design activities for the ship, and projected an additional $852 million in FY2013-FY2017 for acquiring the ship. The Coast Guard's FY2013 budget anticipated awarding a construction contract for the ship "within the next five years" and taking delivery on the ship "within a decade."

FY2014 Budget Submission

The Coast Guard's proposed FY2014 budget requested $2 million in acquisition funding to continue survey and design activities for the ship, or $118 million less than the $120 million that was projected for FY2014 under the FY2013 budget. The Coast Guard's FY2014 budget submission projects an additional $228 million in FY2015-FY2018 for acquiring the ship, including $128 million in FY2015-FY2017, or $604 million less than the $732 million that was projected for FY2015-FY2017 under the Coast Guard's FY2013 budget submission. The Coast Guard's proposed FY2014 budget anticipates awarding a construction contract for the ship "within the next four years." The Coast Guard states that the requested FY2014 funding

> will be used to continue development of programmatic planning documents required under the USCG Major Systems Acquisition Manual, including an Analysis of Alternatives, a Life Cycle Cost Estimate, modeling simulation and testing (as required) to build a modern polar icebreaker. Together with funding provided in 2013, Coast Guard will complete the Mission Needs Statement, the Concept of Operations, and the Preliminary Operational Requirements

---

[39] U.S. Coast Guard, *USCGC POLAR SEA Business Case Analysis, 2103 Report to Congress*, November 7, 2013, p. 4. The report was accessed April 9, 2014, at http://assets.fiercemarkets.net/public/sites/govit/ polarsea_businesscaseanalysis_nov2013.pdf. See also "Second Heavy Icebreaker Not Necessary Through 2022, Says Coast Guard," Fierce Homeland Security (http://www.fiercehomelandsecurity.com), January 19, 2014, which includes a link to the assets fiercemarkets net site at which the report was posted.

Document. These efforts will lead to development of a formal icebreaker acquisition project, with the award for construction anticipated within the next four years.[40]

FY2015 Budget Submission

The Coast Guard's FY2015 budget submission states that the polar icebreaker project received $7.609 million in FY2013 and $2.0 million in FY2014. The Coast Guard's proposed FY2015 budget requests $6 million to continue initial acquisition activities for the ship. The Coast Guard states that the FY2015 funding

> Continues initial activities for a new polar icebreaker, intended to provide continued U.S. Polar icebreaking capability following the projected end of service life of CGC POLAR STAR. This effort will consider requirements analyses undertaken by the Coast Guard within the past several years, including the High-Latitude Mission Analysis Report, and the Polar Icebreaker Business Case Analysis. Additionally, this effort will be informed by the priorities of the U.S. Arctic Region Policy.
>
> This funding will be used to continue development of programmatic planning documents required under the USCG Major Systems Acquisition Manual, including a Life Cycle Cost Estimate and modeling simulation and testing (as required). This funding will also support the development of an initial specification. These efforts will lead to development of a Request for Proposal.
>
> **FY 2013 Key Events**
>
> • Mission Needs Statement Approved;
>
> • Concept of Operations Approved;
>
> • Initial Acquisition Strategy Approved.
>
> **FY 2014 Planned Key Events**
>
> • Capability Development Plan Approval;
>
> • Preliminary Operational Requirements Document Development/Approval;
>
> • Alternatives Analysis Study Plan Approval.
>
> **FY 2015 Planned Key Events**
>
> • Operational Requirements Document Development/Approval;
>
> • Finalize Alternatives Analysis;
>
> • Complete Initial Lifecycle Cost Estimate;
>
> • Conduct Feasibility Studies.[41]

---

[40] Department of Homeland Security, United States Coast Guard, *Fiscal Year 2014 Congressional Justification*, p. CG-AC&I-32 (pdf page 204 of 403).

FY2013, FY2014, and FY2015 Budget Submissions Compared

Table 2 compares funding for the acquisition of a new polar icebreaker under the Coast Guard's FY2013, FY2014, and FY2015 budget submissions.

Table 2. Funding for Acquisition of New Polar Icebreaker Under FY2013, FY2014, and FY2015 Budget Submissions

(millions of then-year dollars)

	FY13	FY14	FY15	FY16	FY17	FY18	FY19
FY2013 budget	8	120	380	270	82		
FY2014 budget		2	8	100	20	100	
FY2015 budget			6	4	100	20	100

Source: Coast Guard FY2013, FY2014, and FY2015 budget submissions.

Issues for Congress

Time Line for Acquiring New Polar Icebreaker

Another potential issue for Congress concerns the time line for acquiring a new polar icebreaker, which appears to have become less certain in the FY2015 budget submission. In the FY2013 budget submission—the submission that initiated the project to acquire the ship—DHS stated that it anticipated awarding a construction contract for the ship "within the next five years" and taking delivery on the ship "within a decade."[42] In the FY2014 budget submission, DHS stated that it anticipated awarding a construction contract for the ship "within the next four years."[43] In the Coast Guard's FY2015 budget-justification book, the entry for the polar icebreaker program does not make a statement as to when a construction contract for the ship might be awarded.[44]

Coast Guard testimony about the icebreaker in 2014 suggests that if the Coast Guard's Acquisition, Construction and Improvement (AC&I) appropriation account remains at about $1 billion per year in coming years (as opposed to some higher figure, such as $1.5 billion per year or $2 billion per year), the icebreaker could become something like an unfunded requirement. For example, at a March 26, 2014, hearing on the proposed FY2015 budgets for the Coast Guard and

---

(...continued)

[41] Department of Homeland Security, United States Coast Guard, *Fiscal Year 2015 Congressional Justification*, p. CG-AC&I-42 (pdf page 196 of 474).

[42] U.S. Department of Homeland Security, *Annual Performance Report, Fiscal Years 2011 – 2013*, p. CG-AC&I-40 (pdf page 1,777 of 3,134).

[43] Department of Homeland Security, United States Coast Guard, *Fiscal Year 2014 Congressional Justification*, p. CG-AC&I-32 (pdf page 204 of 403).

[44] Department of Homeland Security, United States Coast Guard, *Fiscal Year 2015, Congressional Justification*, p. CG-AC&I-42 (pdf page 196 of 474).

maritime transportation programs before the Coast Guard and Maritime Transportation subcommittee of the House Transportation and Infrastructure Committee, Admiral Robert Papp, the Commandant of the Coast Guard at the time, testified that "It's going to be tough to fit a billion dollar icebreaker in our five-year plan without displacing other things," that "I can't afford to pay for an icebreaker in a $1 billion [per year capital investment plan] because it would just displace other things that I have a higher priority for," and that "I still believe firmly, we need to build a new one but we don't have [the] wherewithal right now, but doing the preliminary work should inform decisions that are made three, four, five, maybe 10 years from now."[45]

Number and Capabilities of Future Polar Icebreakers

Factors to Consider

One potential issue for Congress is how many polar icebreakers, with what capabilities, the Coast Guard will need in the future. In assessing this issue, factors that Congress may consider include, but are not limited to, the following:

- current and projected mission demands for Coast Guard polar icebreakers as analyzed in the High Latitude Study and other recent studies, including an assessment of how those demands might be affected by NSF decisions on how to acquire icebreaking services to support its research activities;

- the potential for various mission demands (not just those conducted in support of NSF research activities) to be met by non-Coast Guard icebreakers, including leases or charters of icebreakers owned by foreign governments or private firms; and

- the Coast Guard's overall missions-vs.-resources situation, which includes the Coast Guard's requirements to perform many non-polar missions and the Coast Guard's desire to fund programs for performing these non-polar missions.[46]

Regarding the first factor above, the NSF states that although Coast Guard polar icebreakers are very capable, the NSF is mandated by presidential directive to perform its research activities in the most cost-effective way possible, and that it can be more expensive for NSF to support its research activities with Coast Guard polar icebreakers than with charters of icebreakers crewed by contractor personnel. Although Coast Guard polar icebreakers in the past have performed the annual McMurdo break-in mission, the NSF in certain recent years has chartered Russian and Swedish contractor-operated icebreakers to perform the mission (with a Coast Guard polar icebreaker standing ready to assist if needed). The NSF has also noted that *Healy*, though very capable in supporting Arctic research, operates at sea for about 200 days a year, as opposed to about 300 days a year for foreign contractor-operated polar icebreakers. The Coast Guard states that

> Beginning with Deep Freeze 2008, NSF opted to perform the McMurdo break-in with the Swedish icebreaker ODEN under a five-year contract with the Swedish government. In July 2011, the Government of Sweden cancelled the contract, forcing NSF to contract with

---

[45] Source: Transcript of hearing.

[46] For more on some of these other programs, see CRS Report RL33753, *Coast Guard Deepwater Acquisition Programs: Background, Oversight Issues, and Options for Congress*, by Ronald O'Rourke.

Murmansk Shipping Company for use of the Russian icebreaker VLADIMIR IGNATYUK. NSF awarded a base contract of one year (for Deep Freeze 2012) and two option years, pending POLAR STAR's return to service. NSF exercised one option year for Deep Freeze 2013, and requested POLAR STAR for Deep Freeze 2014. NSF currently intends to use POLAR STAR for 2015 and for the foreseeable future.[47]

Regarding the second factor above, issues to consider would include, among other things, the potential availability of ships for lease, leasing costs, regulatory issues relating to long-term leases of capital assets for the U.S. government, and the ability of leased ships to perform the missions in question, including the mission of defending U.S. sovereignty in Arctic waters north of Alaska, the challenging McMurdo resupply mission, or missions that emerge suddenly in response to unexpected events.[48]

Regarding the first two factors above, some observers note the size of the polar icebreaking fleets operated by other countries. Countries with interests in the polar regions have differing requirements for polar icebreakers, depending on the nature and extent of their polar activities. **Table 3** shows a Coast Guard summary of major icebreakers around the world; the figures in the table include some icebreakers designed for use in the Baltic Sea.

---

[47] Source: Email to CRS from Coast Guard Mobility and Ice Operations Division, April 16, 2014.

[48] The potential for using leased ships, and the possible limitations of this option, are discussed at several points in the 2007 NRC report. The report argues, among other things, that the availability of icebreakers for lease in coming years is open to question, that leased ships are not optimal for performing sovereignty-related operations, and that some foreign icebreakers might be capable of performing the McMurdo resupply mission. See, for example, pages 80-81 of the NRC report. See also Jennifer Scholtes, "In Search of Frozen Assets," *CQ Weekly*, October 10, 2011: 2074.

Table 3. Major Icebreakers Around the World

(as of June 26, 2014)

	Total all types, in inventory (+ under construction + planned)	In inventory, government owned or operated			In inventory, privately owned and operated		
		45,000 or more BHP	20,000 to 44,999 BHP	10,000 to 19,999 BHP	45,000 or more BHP	20,000 to 44,999 BHP	10,000 to 19,999 BHP
Russia	40 (+ 6 + 5)	6 (all nuclear powered; 4 operational)	7	6		12	9
Finland	7 (+ 0 +1)		3	1		3	
Sweden	6		4				2
Canada	6 (+0 +1)		2	4			
United States	5 (+0 +1)	2 (*Polar Star* and *Polar Sea – Polar Sea* not operational)	1 (*Healy*)			1 (*Aiviq* – built for Shell Oil)	1 (*Palmer*)
Denmark	4						4
Estonia	2			2			
Norway	1 (+0 +1)			1			
Germany	1 (+0 +1)			1			
China	1 (+0 +1)			1			
Japan	1		1				
Australia	1			1			
Chile	1			1			
Latvia	1			1			
South Korea	1			1			
South Africa	1			1			
Argentina	1			1 (not operational)			

Source: Table prepared by CRS based on U.S. Coast Guard chart showing data compiled by the Coast Guard as of June 26, 2014, accessed online July 1, 2014, at http://www.uscg.mil/hq/cg5/cg552/ice.asp. The table also lists the United Kingdom as planning one new polar research vessel.

Notes: Includes some icebreakers designed for use in the Baltic Sea. **BHP** = the brake horsepower of the ship's power plant. A ship with 45,000 or more BHP might be considered a heavy polar icebreaker; a ship with 20,000 to 44,999 BHP might be considered a medium polar icebreaker, and a ship with 10,000 to 19,999 BHP might be considered a light polar icebreaker or an ice-capable polar ship.

Notional Arguments for Various Numbers

Advocates of a Coast Guard polar icebreaker fleet that includes two ships—*Healy* plus one heavy polar icebreaker—might argue that the Coast Guard operated with such a force between July 1, 2006 (when *Polar Star* went into caretaker status), until June 2010 (when *Polar Sea* suffered an engine casualty and was removed from service), that the Coast Guard, following the reactivation of *Polar Sea* on December 14, 2012, is once again operating with such a force, and that a force with *Healy* plus one heavy polar icebreaker would cost less than a larger polar icebreaker fleet and thereby permit the Coast Guard to better fund programs for performing its various non-polar missions.

Advocates of a Coast Guard fleet that includes three ships—*Healy* plus two heavy polar icebreakers—might argue that the 2007 NRC report recommended a polar icebreaking fleet of three multimission polar icebreakers (i.e., *Healy* plus two additional polar icebreakers), that the Coast Guard operated with such a force from 2000, when *Healy* entered service, until July 1, 2006, when *Polar Star* went into caretaker status, that the 2006-2010 force of *Healy* and one heavy polar icebreaker made it more difficult for the Coast Guard to perform the McMurdo resupply mission using its own assets, that a force that includes two heavy polar icebreakers rather than one would provide more flexibility for responding to polar contingencies or dealing with mechanical problems on a heavy polar icebreaker, and that such a force would still be sufficiently affordable to permit the Coast Guard to adequately fund programs for performing non-polar missions.

Advocates of a Coast Guard fleet that includes *Healy* plus three heavy polar icebreakers might argue that the High Latitude Study found that the Coast Guard requires three heavy (and three medium) icebreakers to fulfill its statutory missions, that a force with three heavy polar icebreakers would provide additional capability for responding to potentially increased commercial and military activities in the Arctic, that it would more strongly signal U.S. commitment to defending its sovereignty and other interests in the region, and that while such a force would be more expensive than a smaller polar icebreaker fleet, the added investment would be justified in light of the growing focus on U.S. polar interests.

Disposition of *Polar Sea*

Another potential issue for Congress concerns the disposition of *Polar Sea*. As mentioned earlier, Section 222 of the Coast Guard and Maritime Transportation Act of 2012 (H.R. 2838/P.L. 112-213 of December 20, 2012) prohibited the Coast Guard from removing any part of *Polar Sea* and from transferring, relinquishing ownership of, dismantling, or recycling the ship until it submits a business case analysis of the options for and costs of reactivating the ship and extending its service life to at least September 30, 2022, so as to maintain U.S. polar icebreaking capabilities and fulfill the Coast Guard's high latitude mission needs, as identified in the Coast Guard's July 2010, High Latitude Study Mission Analysis Report. As also mentioned earlier, the business case analysis required by Section 222 was submitted to Congress with a cover date of November 7, 2013 (see "Reactivate Polar Sea for Several Years" in "Background.")

Options for the disposition of the ship include the following, among others:

- repairing and reactivating the ship;

- keeping the ship in preservation status in the Maritime Administration's (MARAD's) National Defense Reserve Fleet (NDRF) for potential reactivation to meet increased polar icebreaking needs or to replace *Polar Star*, should that ship be removed from service before the end of its anticipated 7- to 10-year post-reactivation service life due to an accident or the failure of critical equipment that cannot be cost-effectively repaired;

- selling or transferring the ship to another government or to a private owner; and

- dismantling the ship and recycling its scrap metal.

Incremental Funding vs. Full Funding

Another potential issue for Congress concerns the Coast Guard's proposal to fund the acquisition of a new icebreaker using incremental funding (i.e., a series of annual funding increments) rather than full funding (i.e., placing most or all of the ship's acquisition cost into a single year). Section 31.6 of Office of Management and Budget (OMB) Circular A-11[49] normally requires executive branch agencies to use full funding for acquiring capital assets such as a new ship. The Coast Guard appears to have received permission from OMB to propose the use of incremental funding for acquiring a new polar icebreaker; Congress may choose to approve, reject, or modify this proposal.

Supporters of using incremental funding to acquire a new polar icebreaker could argue that funding this ship in a single year would create a one-year "spike" in Coast Guard funding requirements that could require offsetting and potentially disruptive one-year reductions in other Coast Guard programs, and that using incremental funding mitigates the spiking issue by spreading the ship's cost over several years. Supporters could argue that avoiding such budget spikes is a principal reason why the Navy in recent years has been given permission by OMB and Congress to use incremental funding to procure aircraft carriers and amphibious assault ships,[50] and that a polar icebreaker is analogous to an aircraft carrier or an amphibious assault ship in being a very expensive (for the Coast Guard) ship that is procured once every several years.

Supporters of using full funding to acquire a new polar icebreaker could argue that the acquisition cost of a polar icebreaker (roughly $900 million), though large by Coast Guard standards, is much less than that of an aircraft carrier (more than $11 billion) or an amphibious assault ship (more than $3 billion). They could argue that OMB believes using full funding reduces risks in the acquisition of capital assets,[51] and that permitting the use of incremental funding for the procurement of a polar icebreaker could weaken adherence to the policy by setting a precedent for using incremental funding for acquiring other capital assets costing less than $1 billion.

The issue of incremental funding as an alternative to full funding in the acquisition of Navy ships is discussed at length in other CRS reports.[52]

---

[49] The text of OMB Circular A-11 is available online at http://www.whitehouse.gov/omb/circulars_a11_current_year_a11_toc.

[50] See. for example, CRS Report RS20643, *Navy Ford (CVN-78) Class Aircraft Carrier Program: Background and Issues for Congress*, by Ronald O'Rourke.

[51] Appendix J to OMB Circular A-11 states, in explaining the requirement for using full funding, that

> Good budgeting requires that appropriations for the full costs of asset acquisition be enacted in advance to help ensure that all costs and benefits are fully taken into account at the time decisions are made to provide resources. Full funding with regular appropriations in the budget year also leads to tradeoffs within the budget year with spending for other capital assets and with spending for purposes other than capital assets. Full funding increases the opportunity to use performance-based fixed price contracts, allows for more efficient work planning and management of the capital project (or investment), and increases the accountability for the achievement of the baseline goals.

> When full funding is not followed and capital projects (or investments) or useful segments are funded in increments, without certainty if or when future funding will be available, the result is sometimes poor planning, acquisition of assets not fully justified, higher acquisition costs, cancellation of major investments, the loss of sunk costs, or inadequate funding to maintain and operate the assets.

[52] See CRS Report RL31404, *Defense Procurement: Full Funding Policy—Background, Issues, and Options for Congress*, by Ronald O'Rourke and Stephen Daggett, and CRS Report RL32776, *Navy Ship Procurement: Alternative* (continued...)

Funding Ships in Coast Guard Budget or Elsewhere

Another potential issue for Congress, if it is determined that one or more new icebreakers should be procured by the government through a traditional acquisition, is whether the acquisition cost of those ships should be funded entirely through Coast Guard's Acquisition, Construction, and Improvements (AC&I) account, or partly or entirely through other parts of the federal budget, such as the Department of Defense (DOD) budget, the NSF budget, or both.[53] Within the DOD budget, possibilities include the Navy's shipbuilding account, called the Shipbuilding and Conversion, Navy (SCN) account, and the National Defense Sealift Fund (NDSF), which is an account where DOD sealift ships and Navy auxiliary ships are funded.

There is precedent for funding Coast Guard icebreakers in the DOD budget: The procurement of *Healy* was funded in FY1990 in the DOD budget—specifically, the SCN account.[54] Advocates of funding new icebreakers partly or entirely through the SCN account or the NDSF might argue that this could permit the funding of new icebreakers while putting less pressure on other parts of the Coast Guard's budget. They might also argue that it would permit the new icebreaker program to benefit from the Navy's experience in managing shipbuilding programs. Opponents might argue that funding new icebreakers in the SCN account or the NDSF might put pressure on these other two accounts at a time when the Navy and DOD are facing challenges funding their own shipbuilding and other priorities. They might also argue that having the Navy manage the Coast Guard's icebreaker program would add complexity to the acquisition effort, and that it is unclear whether the Navy's recent performance in managing shipbuilding programs is better than the Coast Guard's, since both services have recently experienced problems in managing shipbuilding programs—the Coast Guard with the procurement of new Deepwater cutters, and the Navy in the Littoral Combat Ship (LCS) program and the LPD-17 class amphibious ship program.[55]

At a March 12, 2014, hearing on the Coast Guard's proposed FY2015 budget before the Homeland Security subcommittee of the House Appropriations Committee, the Commandant of the Coast at the time, Admiral Robert Papp stated:

> What concerns me, however, is—particularly as I'm being constrained closer to the billion-dollar range in my acquisition projects [i.e., the Coast Guard's Acquisition, Construction, and Improvements, or AC&I, account], I don't—I don't know how you fit in a billion-dollar icebreaker. Because at some point, you're going to have to take—even if you do it with a multi-year strategy [i.e., incremental funding], you're going to have go $300 billion [sic:

(...continued)

Funding Approaches—Background and Options for Congress, by Ronald O'Rourke.

[53] For more on the NSF, whose budget is normally funded through the annual Commerce, Justice, Science, and Related Agencies appropriations bill, see CRS Report 95-307, *U.S. National Science Foundation: An Overview*, by Christine M. Matthews.

[54] The FY1990 DOD appropriations act (II.R. 3072/P.L. 101-165 of November 21, 1989) provided $329 million for the procurement of *Healy* in the SCN account. (See pages 77 and 78 of H.Rept. 101-345 of November 13, 1989). The NDSF was created three years later, in FY1993, as a fund for procuring DOD sealift ships, among other purposes, and since FY2001 has been used to fund Navy auxiliary ships as well.

[55] For more on Deepwater acquisition programs and the LCS and LPD-17 programs, see CRS Report RL33753, *Coast Guard Deepwater Acquisition Programs: Background, Oversight Issues, and Options for Congress*, by Ronald O'Rourke; CRS Report RL33741, *Navy Littoral Combat Ship (LCS) Program: Background and Issues for Congress*, by Ronald O'Rourke; and CRS Report RL34476, *Navy LPD-17 Amphibious Ship Procurement: Background, Issues, and Options for Congress*, by Ronald O'Rourke.

million] or $400 billion [sic: million] in a couple of years, which would displace other very important things.

So, we're having to take a hard look at this. One way of doing it is to say, OK, this icebreaker serves the interagency. The Department of Defense could call on us. NSF certainly does, and other agencies. Why should that not be a shared expense?

And, oh, by the way, if all these companies are going to be making that much money off oil exploration and the arctic, maybe they can share in the cost of this icebreaker.[56]

A moment later in the hearing, Papp also stated:

And I know the president has committed us to designing an icebreaker. We haven't committed to building an icebreaker yet. And if I'm constrained at a billion dollars [per year in the AC&I account], I just don't know how you do it. Because I have higher priorities to build within that—that AC&I money.[57]

Similarly, at a March 26, 2014, hearing on the proposed FY2015 budget for the Coast Guard and maritime transportation programs before the Coast Guard and Maritime Transportation subcommittee of the House Transportation and Infrastructure Committee, Papp stated, in response to a question about the Coast Guard's five-year capital investment plan (CIP), that

we're facing the need for icebreaker for the United States. It's going to be tough to fit a billion dollar icebreaker in our five-year plan without displacing other things.

If there's going to be no growth in the budget and that's what I have to plan for right now, I need to address those highest priorities that I have but rightly so, there are other people who have opinions with an opening Arctic and other things that perhaps, an icebreaker ought to be a higher priority.

These things needed to be negotiated out and then come to an administration's position on what the highest priorities are. I'm hopeful that the priorities that I see for the Coast Guard will be reflected in that SIP [sic: CIP] when it gets up here.[58]

A moment later in the hearing, he also stated:

I can't afford to pay for an icebreaker in a 1-billion-dollar [per year] SIP [sic: CIP] because it would just displace other things that I have a higher priority for.

So we're looking at other alternatives, perhaps one of those alternatives, the Congress came up with a requirement for a business base analysis on the remaining Polar Seal [sic: Sea] icebreaker, Polar Sea and potentially, we might be able to overhaul Polar Sea and fit that into the SIP [sic: CIP] as an affordable means for providing an additional icebreaker as we await a time that we can build a new icebreaker.

If we are going to build a new icebreaker, if that is a priority, we just can't fit it within our acquisition account and I would look across the inter-agency [for the funding].[59]

---

[56] Transcript of hearing.

[57] Transcript of hearing.

[58] Transcript of hearing.

[59] Transcript of hearing.

Later in the hearing, he stated:

> The Offshore Patrol Cutter is my highest priority for the Coast Guard. I need to fit that in the budget and I fear that if we try to fit the cost of an icebreaker in there, it would displace the Offshore Patrol Cutter or some other very important things. So my number one option is to get support across the inter-agency, those agencies that benefit from the support of an icebreaker to contribute towards the construction of it, that would be my first choice.
>
> My second choice however, when I start looking at what can I fit within our acquisition budget refurbishment of the Polar Sea maybe a viable option for that. I would say what you would want to do is overlap and so as Polar Star is coming towards the end of that decade of service after refurbishment, we have polar—I think I said Polar Star.[60]

The Coast Guard states on its Internet page for the polar icebreaker program that

> In order to fully fund subsequent phases of this project, the Coast Guard believes that a "whole-of-government" approach will be necessary. Obtaining a new, heavy polar icebreaker that meets Coast Guard requirements will depend upon supplementary financing from other agencies whose activities also rely upon the nation possessing a robust, Arctic-capable surface fleet.[61]

The prepared statement of the GAO witness at a December 1, 2011, hearing before the Coast Guard and Maritime Transportation subcommittee of the House Transportation and Infrastructure Committee that focused primarily on icebreakers states:

> Another alternative option addressed by the Recapitalization report would be to fund new icebreakers through the NSF. However, the analysis of this option concluded that funding a new icebreaker through the existing NSF budget would have significant adverse impacts on NSF operations and that the capability needed for Coast Guard requirements would exceed that needed by the NSF.
>
> The Recapitalization report noted that a funding approach similar to the approach used for the Healy, which was funded through the fiscal year 1990 DOD appropriations, should be considered. However, the report did not analyze the feasibility of this option. We have previously reported that because of the Coast Guard's statutory role as both a federal maritime agency and a branch of the military, it can receive funding through both the Department of Homeland Security (DHS) and DOD. For example, as we previously reported, although the U.S. Navy is not expressly required to provide funding to the Coast Guard, the Coast Guard receives funding from the Navy to purchase and maintain equipment, such as self-defense systems or communication systems, because it is in the Navy's interest for the Coast Guard systems to be compatible with the Navy's systems when the Coast Guard is performing national defense missions in support of the Navy. However, according to a Coast Guard budget official, the Coast Guard receives the majority of its funding through the DHS appropriation, with the exception of reimbursements for specific activities. Also, as the Recapitalization plan acknowledges, there is considerable strain on the DOD budget. A recent DOD report on the Arctic also notes budgetary challenges, stating that the near-term fiscal and political environment will make it difficult to support significant new U.S. investments in the Arctic. Furthermore, DOD and the Coast Guard face different

---

[60] Transcript of hearing.

[61] Coast Guard Internet page entitled "Icebreaker," accessed April 9, 2014, at http://www.uscg mil/ACQUISITION/ icebreaker/default.asp. See also Yasmin Tadjdeh, "Pressure Builds for New Polar Icebreaker," *National Defense (www.nationaldefensemagazine.org)*, February 2014.

mission requirements and timelines. For example, DOD's recent report states that the current level of human activity in the Arctic is already of concern to DHS, whereas the Arctic is expected to remain a peripheral interest to much of the national security community for the next decade or more. As a result, the Coast Guard has a more immediate need than DOD to acquire Arctic capabilities, such as icebreakers. For example, with preliminary plans for drilling activity approved in 2011, the Coast Guard must be prepared to provide environmental response in the event of an oil spill. Similarly, as cruise ship traffic continues to increase, the Coast Guard must be prepared to conduct search and rescue operations should an incident occur. For these reasons, it is unlikely that an approach similar to the one that was used to build the Healy would be feasible at this time.[62]

New Construction vs. Service Life Extension

Another potential issue for Congress is whether requirements for polar icebreakers over the next 25 to 30 years should be met by building new ships, by extending the service lives of existing polar icebreakers, or by pursuing some combination of these options. In assessing this question, factors to consider include the relative costs of these options, the capabilities that each option would provide, the long-term supportability of older ships whose service lives have been extended, and industrial-base impacts.

Regarding relative costs, as discussed in the "Background" section, the Coast Guard estimates that new icebreakers with a 30-year design life might cost $800 million to $925 million per ship in 2008 dollars, while a 25-year service life extension of *Polar Star* and *Polar Sea* might cost about $400 million per ship in 2008 dollars,[63] and repairing and reactivating *Polar Sea* for 7 to 10 years of operation might cost about $100 million. These estimates, however, should be compared with caution: the estimate for building new ships depends in part on the capabilities that were assumed for those ships, and estimates for service-life extension work can be very uncertain due to the potential for discovering new things about a ship's condition once the ship is opened up for service-life-extension work.

Regarding capabilities provided by each option, the new-construction option would provide entirely new ships with extensive use of new technology, while the service-life-extension option would provide ships that, although modernized and reconditioned, would not be entirely new and would likely make less extensive use of new technologies. Among other things, new-construction ships might be able to make more extensive use of new technologies for reducing crew size, which is a significant factor in a ship's life cycle operating and support costs.

Regarding long-term supportability of older ships, the Coast Guard has expressed concern about the ability to support ships whose service lives have been extended after FY2014, because some contracts that currently provide that support are scheduled to end that year.[64]

---

[62] Government Accountability Office, *Coast Guard[:] Observations on Arctic Requirements, Icebreakers, and Coordination with Stakeholders, Testimony Before the Subcommittee on Coast Guard and Maritime Transportation, Committee on Transportation and Infrastructure, House of Representatives, Statement of Stephen L. Caldwell, Director, Homeland Security and Justice*, GAO-12-254T, December 1, 2011, pp. 24-25.

[63] As mentioned earlier, an August 30, 2010, press report stated that the Commandant of the Coast Guard at the time, Admiral Robert Papp, estimated the cost of extending the lives of Polar Star and Polar Sea at about $500 million per ship. (Cid Standifer, "Papp: Refurbished Icebreaker Hulls Could Last 'An Awful Long Time,'" *Inside the Navy*, August 30, 2010.)

[64] CRS discussion with Coast Guard officials, January 30, 2008.

Regarding potential impact on the industrial base, repair and reactivation work and service life extensions would likely provide shipyards and supplier firms with less work, and also exercise a smaller set of shipyard construction skills, than would building new ships.

A June 18, 2014, press report states:

> The U.S. Coast Guard's No. 2 commander said refurbishing the aging Polar Sea icebreaker now idled in Seattle would allow it to meet the nation's Arctic mission for the next decade until a replacement ship can be built.
>
> The comment Wednesday by Vice Admiral Peter Neffenger is the Coast Guard's clearest endorsement yet for fixing up the 1970s-era Polar Sea, which in 2012 was on the verge of being decommissioned and used for spare parts for its sister ship, the Polar Star.
>
> In an interview at a seminar on Arctic shipping hosted by the Royal Norwegian Embassy in Washington, D.C., Neffenger said salvaging the Polar Sea would be a "viable alternative" to a new heavy-duty icebreaker that could cost up to $1 billion.
>
> "We think that would be adequate (to meet the mission) for the next 10 years," Neffenger said.
>
> In March, then-Admiral Robert Papp offered a more tepid embrace during a congressional hearing. Papp testified that returning the Polar Sea to service was an option, but noted for the record that "I didn't say a good option."
>
> Neffenger, who began serving as vice commandant in May, said retrofitting the Polar Sea would be a stopgap solution. It can take a decade to build a new icebreaker, and the United States needs to act quickly.
>
> "That window is now," he said.[65]

Procurement vs. Leasing

Another potential issue for Congress is whether future polar icebreakers should be acquired through a traditional acquisition (i.e., the government procuring the ship and owning it throughout its service life) or through a leasing arrangement (under which the icebreakers would be privately built and privately owned, leased to the Coast Guard, and crewed by an all-Coast Guard crew or a mix of Coast Guard personnel and civilian mariners). Factors to consider in assessing this issue include the comparative costs of the two options and the potential differences between them in terms of factors such as average number of days of operation each year and capability for performing various missions. Comparing the potential costs of leasing versus purchasing a capital asset often involves, among other things, calculating the net present value of each option.

At a December 1, 2011, hearing before the Coast Guard and Maritime Transportation subcommittee of the House Transportation and Infrastructure Committee that focused on the polar icebreaker fleet, Admiral Robert Papp, the Commandant of the Coast Guard at the time, stated:

---

[65] Kyung M. Song, "Coast Guard Makes Case to Refurbish Idled Icebreaker," *Seattle Times (http://seattletimes.com)*, June 18, 2014.

As far as we can determine, there are no icebreakers available—no heavy icebreakers available for leasing right now. They would have to be constructed [and then leased].

If we were to lease an icebreaker, I'm sure that a company building an icebreaker outside of the government does not have to contend with the same federal acquisition rules that we have to if we were to construct an icebreaker. It could probably be done quicker.

Personally, I'm ambivalent in terms of how we get an icebreaker for the Coast Guard. We've done the legal research. If we lease an icebreaker, we can put a Coast Guard crew on it and still have it as a U.S. vessel supporting U.S. sovereignty.

But the—but they aren't available right now. And the other challenge that we face is the federal acquisition rules and [Office of Management and Budget Circular] A-11 requirements that [direct how to] score the money [in the budget] for leasing. We'd have to put up a significant amount of upfront money even with a lease that we don't have room for within our budget currently.[66]

At another point in the hearing, Admiral Papp stated:

We have looked at various business case scenarios, each and every time looking at, once again, from our normal perspective, the Coast Guard perspective, which has been owning ships forever. And generally, we keep ships 30-40 years or beyond. There is a point where leasing becomes more expensive, it's at or about the 20-25-year timeline.

I just don't have the experience with leasing to be able to give you a good opinion on it. And once again, I'm ambivalent. We just need the icebreaking capability, I think it's for people who can do the analysis, the proper analysis of—but also have to take into account the capabilities required and we need to get about the business of determining the exact capabilities that we need which would take into account National Science Foundation requirements, Coast Guard requirements, requirements to break-in at McMurdo, to come up with a capable ship.[67]

At another point in the hearing, he stated:

As I said, sir, I am truly ambivalent to this except from what I experienced. I do have now two points, yes the Navy leases some ships, but we've got a Navy that has well over 300 ships.

So if they lose a leased vessel or something is pulled back or something happens, they have plenty of other ships they can fall back upon. Right now, all I am falling back on is the Coast Guard cutter Healy. And it feels good to know that we own that and that is our ship for 30 or 40 years and we can rely upon it.

In terms of leasing, I don't know. My personal experience is I lease one of my two cars and I pay a lot of money leasing my car. But at the end of the lease period, I have no car and I've spent a lot of money. So I don't know if that's directly applicable to ships as well, but right now I got half my garage is empty because I just turned one in.[68]

---

[66] Source: Transcript of hearing.

[67] Source: Transcript of hearing.

[68] Source: Transcript of hearing.

At another point in the hearing, he stated:

> We've looked through the legal considerations on this, as long as we have a Coast Guard crew. In fact, you can even make a mixed crew of civilians and Coast Guard people. But as long as it's commanding by—commanded by [a] commissioned officer, you can assert sovereignty, you can take it into war zones and, in fact, the Navy does that as well.[69]

Another witness at the hearing—Mead Treadwell, the lieutenant governor of Alaska—stated:

> [Regarding] The issue of the ships, the company that is building these ships for Shell [Oil] has visited with me and other state officials, and that's why you heard us say in our testimony that we think the leasing option should be considered. We don't have a way to judge the relative cost. But if on the face of it, it seems like it may be a way to get us the capability that the admiral needs.[70]

Another witness at the hearing—Jeffrey Garrett, a retired Coast Guard admiral who spent much of his career on polar icebreakers—stated:

> The perspective I could offer was when I was a member of the Cameron [sic: Commandant's?] staff back in the last '80s here in Washington, we were directed to pursue exactly the same sort of lease versus buy analysis, and in fact, the Coast Guard had a two track procurement strategy to compare leasing a new Polar icebreaker or buying it.
>
> And after over a year of analysis, studies, discussion with other agencies looking around, what became clear was, number one, there was no off-the-shelf asset readily available. And secondly, that in the long run, if you—when you cost it all out and the value of the stream of payments, leasing would actually cost more.
>
> And when we did the recapitalization analysis recently, we also reviewed leasing again, and the I think the findings in that report indicate more expensive over the life of the vessel by about 12 percent.[71]

When asked why this was the finding, Garrett stated:

> A couple of technical things. First of all, whoever builds the ship—and again, this will have to be ship built for the Coast Guard since there's not something off-the-shelf out there that you could lease. Whoever builds it has to raise capital, and nobody can raise capital more inexpensively than the federal government.
>
> Secondly, whoever leases the ship is obviously going to make—want to make a profit on that lease. So just like as Admiral Papp referred to leasing your car, you know, there's going to be a profit involved. And so, if you take the net present value of all of those, of those payments, you got come out with the more expensive package for the same, if you're comparing the same vessel.

---

[69] Source: Transcript of hearing.

[70] Source: Transcript of hearing. The transcript reviewed by CRS attributes this quote to the GAO witness, Stephen Caldwell, but this appears to be a mistake, as the statement is made by a member of the first witness panel, which included the Commandant of the Coast Guard and the Lieutenant Governor. The GAO witness was a member of the second witness panel. The reference in the quote to "me and other state officials" indicates that the witness speaking was the Lieutenant Governor and not the Commandant.

[71] Source: Transcript of hearing.

The other, the other issue I think is more intangible and that's just the fact that we're really not talking about an auxiliary like the Naval, like the Navy leases a supply ship or something like that. We're talking about a frontline Coast Guard capital asset, if you will, capital ship that's going to be doing frontline government missions projecting U.S. sovereignty.

And you know, the Navy doesn't lease those kinds of ships for its frontline fleet and the Coast Guard doesn't lease those kinds of ships for its mission capabilities, and that's what we're really talking about in terms of the ship we need here.

So while a lease may look attractive, I think there are several things that indicate it may not be the right way to go. And the—I think that's what we came down to. And again, this is all documented in the past and that late '80s analysis was re-summarizing the president's 1990 report to Congress which basically says leasing is more expensive and it's not the way to go for a new ship. That was the ship that actually became the Healy then.[72]

The prepared statement of Stephen Caldwell, the GAO witness at the hearing, states:

> The three reports discussed earlier in this [GAO] statement all identify funding as a central issue in addressing the existing and anticipated challenges related to icebreakers. In addition to the Coast Guard budget analysis included in the Recapitalization report, all three reports reviewed alternative financing options, including the potential for leasing icebreakers, or funding icebreakers through the National Science Foundation (NSF) or the Department of Defense (DOD). Although DOD has used leases and charters in the past when procurement funding levels were insufficient to address mission requirements and capabilities, both the Recapitalization report and the High Latitude Study determined that the lack of existing domestic commercial vessels capable of meeting the Coast Guard's mission requirements reduces the availability of leasing options for the Coast Guard. Additionally, an initial cost-benefit analysis of one type of available leasing option included in the Recapitalization report and the High Latitude Study suggests that it may ultimately be more costly to the Coast Guard over the 30-year icebreaker lifespan.[73]

Legislative Activity for FY2015

FY2015 Funding Request

The Coast Guard's proposed FY2015 budget requests $6 million to continue initial acquisition activities for a new polar icebreaker.

Coast Guard and Maritime Transportation Act of 2014 (H.R. 4005)

H.R. 4005 was introduced on February 6, 2014, reported (amended) by the House Transportation and Infrastructure Committee on March 25, 2014 (H.Rept. 113-384 of March 25, 2014), and

---

[72] Source: Transcript of hearing.

[73] Government Accountability Office, *Coast Guard[:] Observations on Arctic Requirements, Icebreakers, and Coordination with Stakeholders, Testimony Before the Subcommittee on Coast Guard and Maritime Transportation, Committee on Transportation and Infrastructure, House of Representatives, Statement of Stephen L. Caldwell, Director, Homeland Security and Justice*, GAO-12-254T, December 1, 2011, p. 24.

agreed to as amended by the House by voice vote on April 1, 2014. **Section 214** of the bill as agreed to by the House states:

SEC. 214. ICEBREAKERS.

(a) Coast Guard Polar Icebreakers- Section 222 of the Coast Guard and Maritime Transportation Act of 2012 (P.L. 112-213; 126 Stat. 1560)[74] is amended—

---

[74] The text of Section 222 of H.R. 2838/P.L. 112-213 of December 20, 2012, the Coast Guard and Maritime Transportation Act of 2012, is as follows:

SEC. 222. COAST GUARD POLAR ICEBREAKERS.

(a) In General- The Secretary of the department in which the Coast Guard is operating shall conduct a business case analysis of the options for and costs of reactivating and extending the service life of the Polar Sea until at least September 30, 2022, to maintain United States polar icebreaking capabilities and fulfill the Coast Guard's high latitude mission needs, as identified in the Coast Guard's July 2010, High Latitude Study Mission Analysis Report, during the Coast Guard's recapitalization of its polar class icebreaker fleet. The analysis shall include—

(1) an assessment of the current condition of the Polar Sea;

(2) a determination of the Polar Sea's operational capabilities with respect to fulfilling the Coast Guard's high latitude operating requirements if renovated and reactivated;

(3) a detailed estimate of costs with respect to reactivating and extending the service life of the Polar Sea;

(4) a life cycle cost estimate with respect to operating and maintaining the Polar Sea for the duration of its extended service life; and

(5) a determination of whether it is cost-effective to reactivate the Polar Sea compared with other options to provide icebreaking services as part of a strategy to maintain polar icebreaking services.

(b) Restrictions- The Secretary shall not remove any part of the Polar Sea until the Secretary submits the analysis required under subsection (a).

(c) Deadline- Not later than 270 days after the date of enactment of this Act, the Secretary shall submit to the Committee on Transportation and Infrastructure of the House of Representatives and the Committee on Commerce, Science, and Transportation of the Senate the analysis required under subsection (a).

(d) Requirement for Reactivation of Polar Sea-

(1) SERVICE LIFE EXTENSION PLAN-

(A) IN GENERAL- If the Secretary determines based on the analysis required under subsection (a) that it is cost-effective to reactivate the Polar Sea compared with other options to provide icebreaking services, the Secretary shall develop a service life extension plan for such reactivation, including a timetable for such reactivation.

(B) UTILIZATION OF EXISTING RESOURCES- In the development of the plan required under subparagraph (A), the Secretary shall utilize to the greatest extent practicable recent plans, studies, assessments, and analyses regarding the Coast Guard's icebreakers and high latitude mission needs and operating requirements.

(C) SUBMISSION- The Secretary shall submit the plan required under subparagraph (A), if so required, to the Committee on Transportation and Infrastructure of the House of Representatives and the Committee on Commerce, Science, and Transportation of the Senate not later than 180 days after the submission of the analysis required under subsection (a).

(2) DECOMMISSIONING; BRIDGING STRATEGY- If the analysis required under subsection (a) is submitted in accordance with subsection (c) and the Secretary determines under subsection (a)(5) that it is not cost-effective to reactivate the Polar Sea, then not later than 180 days after the date on which the analysis is required to be submitted under subsection (c) the Commandant of the Coast Guard—

(A) may decommission the Polar Sea; and

(B) shall submit a bridging strategy for maintaining the Coast Guard's polar icebreaking services (continued...)

---

(1) in subsection (d)(2)—

(A) in the paragraph heading by striking `; BRIDGING STRATEGY'; and

(B) by striking `Commandant of the Coast Guard' and all that follows through the period at the end and inserting `Commandant of the Coast Guard may decommission the Polar Sea.';

(2) by adding at the end of subsection (d) the following:

`(3) RESULT OF NO DETERMINATION- If in the analysis submitted under this section the Secretary does not make a determination under subsection (a)(5) regarding whether it is cost-effective to reactivate the Polar Sea, then—

`(A) the Commandant of the Coast Guard may decommission the Polar Sea; or

`(B) the Secretary may make such determination, not later than 90 days after the date of enactment of this paragraph, and take actions in accordance with this subsection as though such determination was made in the analysis previously submitted.';

(3) by redesignating subsections (e), (f), and (g) as subsections (f), (g), and (h), respectively; and

(4) by inserting after subsection (d) the following:

`(e) Strategies-

`(1) IN GENERAL- Not later than 180 days after the date on which the analysis required under subsection (a) is submitted, the Commandant of the Coast Guard shall submit to the Committee on Transportation and Infrastructure of the House of Representatives and the Committee on Commerce, Science, and Transportation of the Senate—

(...continued)

until at least September 30, 2022, to the Committee on Transportation and Infrastructure of the House of Representatives and the Committee on Commerce, Science, and Transportation of the Senate.

(e) Restriction- Except as provided in subsection (d), the Commandant of the Coast Guard may not—

(1) transfer, relinquish ownership of, dismantle, or recycle the Polar Sea or Polar Star;

(2) change the current homeport of either of the vessels; or

(3) expend any funds—

(A) for any expenses directly or indirectly associated with the decommissioning of either of the vessels, including expenses for dock use or other goods and services;

(B) for any personnel expenses directly or indirectly associated with the decommissioning of either of the vessels, including expenses for a decommissioning officer;

(C) for any expenses associated with a decommissioning ceremony for either of the vessels;

(D) to appoint a decommissioning officer to be affiliated with either of the vessels; or

(E) to place either of the vessels in inactive status.

(f) Definition- For purposes of this section—

(1) the term `Polar Sea' means Coast Guard Cutter Polar Sea (WAGB 11); and

(2) the term `Polar Star' means Coast Guard Cutter Polar Star (WAGB 10).

(g) Repeal- This section shall cease to have effect on September 30, 2022.

`(A) a strategy to meet the Coast Guard's Arctic ice operations needs through September 30, 2050; and

`(B) unless the Secretary makes a determination under this section that it is cost-effective to reactivate the Polar Sea, a bridging strategy for maintaining the Coast Guard's polar icebreaking services until at least September 30, 2024.

`(2) REQUIREMENT- The strategies required under paragraph (1) shall include a business case analysis comparing the leasing and purchasing of icebreakers to maintain the needs and services described in that paragraph.'.

(b) Limitation-

(1) IN GENERAL- The Secretary of the department in which the Coast Guard is operating may not expend amounts appropriated for the Coast Guard for any of fiscal years 2015 through 2024, for—

(A) design activities related to a capability of a Polar-Class Icebreaker that is based on an operational requirement of another Federal department or agency, except for amounts appropriated for design activities for a fiscal year before fiscal year 2016; or

(B) long-lead-time materials, production, or post-delivery activities related to such a capability.

(2) OTHER AMOUNTS- Amounts made available to the Secretary under an agreement with another Federal department or agency and expended on a capability of a Polar-Class Icebreaker that is based on an operational requirement of that or another Federal department or agency shall not be treated as amounts expended by the Secretary for purposes of the limitation established under paragraph (1).

Regarding Section 214, H.Rept. 113-384 states:

> *Sec. 214. Icebreakers*
>
> This section requires the Coast Guard to provide the Committee with a strategy to maintain icebreaking capabilities in the Polar Regions that includes an analysis of the cost effectiveness of acquiring or leasing new icebreaker assets. The section also prohibits the Coast Guard from spending any of its funds to pay for the capabilities of a new Polar Class icebreaker that are requested by other federal agencies. The Coast Guard is authorized to use funds transferred from other agencies pursuant to an agreement to address such requests. (Page 36)

FY2015 DHS Appropriations Act (H.R. 4903/S. 2534)

House

The House Appropriations Committee, in its report (H.Rept. 113-481 of June 19, 2014) on H.R. 4903, recommends reducing to zero the Coast Guard's request for $6 million in FY2015 acquisition funding for a new polar icebreaker (page 79). H.Rept. 113-481 states that this recommendation is "due to excessive carryover of funding from prior years" in the polar icebreaker program (page 78). The report also states:

Polar Ice Breaker Vessel

The Committee recommends no additional funding for the polar icebreaker program, a decrease of $6,000,000 from the request, and $2,000,000 below the amount provided in fiscal year 2014. The Committee has long sought a solution to address this much needed capability. However, since the polar icebreaker effort was initiated in fiscal year 2013, the Coast Guard has obligated merely $1,700,000 of the $10,000,000 that has been appropriated over the last two fiscal years. Based on the current obligation rate, the program can continue without delay through fiscal year 2015 with the funds that have been previously appropriated.

To date, this Administration has failed repeatedly to present a viable acquisition program for a new icebreaker. Previous CIPs have alluded to an incrementally funded acquisition within the existing Coast Guard AC&I topline funding level—a topline that has apparently been set arbitrarily with no relation to Coast Guard requirements. These proposals may partially fund an icebreaker, but only at the expense of existing, validated Coast Guard recapitalization programs. This type of artifice is needless and it senselessly jeopardizes the future of the Coast Guard.

It would also be unreasonable for the Administration to impose the entire cost of an icebreaker on the Coast Guard because its mission, in part, is tied to the missions and requirements of other executive branch agencies, and these requirements will add significantly to the total cost of the asset. The Committee believes that for a national asset of this type, shared funding among stakeholder agencies is a more appropriate and fair method of funding—allowing for continued recapitalization of the Coast Guard while at the same time acquiring a long needed icebreaking capability. (Pages 80-81)

Senate

The Senate Appropriations Committee, in its report (S.Rept. 113-198 of June 26, 2013) on S. 2534, recommends approving the Coast Guard's request for $6 million in FY2015 acquisition funding for a new polar icebreaker (page 89). The report also recommends an additional $8 million for preserving the material condition of *Polar Sea*. S.Rept. 113-198 states:

POLAR ICEBREAKER

The recommendation includes $6,000,000, as requested, to continue survey and design activities for a new Coast Guard polar icebreaker.

The Coast Guard's High Latitude Study calls for a minimum of three new heavy icebreakers to address increased activity in the Arctic region, protect our national interests, and provide search and rescue in emergency maritime situations. Currently, the Coast Guard operates one medium service icebreaker, the Healy, which is used primarily for scientific missions in the Arctic and one heavy polar icebreaker, the Polar Star, which was recently reactivated in 2013 and is estimated to remain operational for a total of 7–10 years. The service's other heavy polar icebreaker, the Polar Sea, is out of service based on its mechanical state. Based on the Coast Guard's projected acquisition timeline for a new heavy polar icebreaker, the earliest date in which a fully operational vessel can be deployed is 2026–2028, which leaves a potential gap of time where no heavy polar icebreaker will be available. Therefore, the Committee recommendation includes $8,000,000 to preserve the material condition of the Polar Sea in anticipation of future reactivation. Not later than 30 days after the date of enactment of this act, the Coast Guard is to brief the Committee on all expenditures and associated timelines to perform the work associated with vessel preservation. (Page 92)

S.Rept. 113-198 also states:

POLAR ICEBREAKER

The Committee is concerned about the lack of icebreakers available for the Coast Guard's missions. No later than July 31, 2015, the Coast Guard is directed to brief the Committee on the Operational Requirements Document and Alternatives Analysis with respect to initial funding, timeline, and vessel specifications related to the construction of a new Polar-class icebreaker. The Coast Guard will further brief the Committee on the Department's plans to ensure deployment of a new heavy icebreaker prior to decommissioning of the Polar Star and Polar Sea. In assessing needs for an Arctic-capable fleet, the Secretary is encouraged to focus on the Coast Guard's statutory missions, including search and rescue, ice operations, law enforcement, aids to navigation, marine safety, marine environmental protection, living marine resources, ports, waterways and coastal security, defense readiness, migrant interdiction, and drug interdiction. (Page 85)

Author Contact Information

Ronald O'Rourke
Specialist in Naval Affairs
rorourke@crs.loc.gov, 7-7610